WINNING SOULS THE BIBLE WAY

WILLIAM MACDONALD

Developed as a study course by Emmaus Correspondence School, founded in 1942.

ECS Ministries exists to glorify God by providing biblically-sound resources and structured study materials for the purpose of teaching people from every nation to know Jesus Christ as Savior and to live in a way that is consistent with God's Word.

Winning Souls the Bible Way
William MacDonald
Published by:
 Emmaus Correspondence School
 (A division of ECS Ministries)
 PO Box 1028
 Dubuque, IA 52004-1028
 phone: (563) 585-2070
 email: ecsorders@ecsministries.org
 website: www.ecsministries.org

First Printed 2010 (AK '10), 1 Unit
Reprinted 2014 (AK '10), 1 Unit
Reprinted 2017 (AK '10), 1 Unit
ISBN 978-1-59387-120-8
Code: WSBW
Copyright © 2010 William MacDonald

Many Bible study courses may also be taken via smart phones, tablets, and computers. For more information, visit the ECS website www.ecsministries.org

All rights in this course are reserved. No part of this publication may be reproduced or transmitted in any manner, electronic or mechanical, including photocopy, recording, or any information storage and retrieval system including the Internet without written permission from the publisher. Permission is not needed for brief quotations embodied in critical articles and reviews.

All Scripture quotations, unless otherwise indicated, are taken from the New King James Version. Copyright © 1979, 1980, 1982 by Thomas Nelson, Inc. Used by permission. All rights reserved.

Printed in the United States of America

Student Instructions

One of the greatest privileges of the Christian believer is to be associated with God in the important work of winning souls to the Lord Jesus Christ. This course will prepare you for this by providing guidance about personal responsibility, how to use God's Word, the role of the Holy Spirit, presenting the gospel, challenges and difficulties, follow-up, and other important areas. After you complete the course you will be ready to win souls "the Bible way."

Lessons You Will Study

1. Why Personal Evangelism? 5
2. Personal Preparation for Soul Winning 9
3. The Soul Winner's Weapon 13
4. The Ministry of the Holy Spirit 17
5. Lessons from the Gospels and the Book of Acts 21
6. Conviction of Sin 25
7. The True Gospel 29
8. Belief and Confession 34
9. The Assurance of Salvation 38
10. Other Perplexing Problems 41
11. Follow-Up Work 46
12. Discipleship 49

Course Components

This course has two parts: this study course and the exam booklet.

How To Study

This study has twelve chapters, and each chapter has its own exam. Begin by asking God to help you understand the material. Read the chapter through at least twice, once to get a general idea of its contents and then again, slowly, looking up any Bible references given.

Begin studying immediately, or if you are in a group, as soon as the group begins. We suggest that you keep a regular schedule by trying to complete at least one chapter per week.

Exams

In the exam booklet there is one exam for each chapter (exam 1 covers chapter 1 of the course). Do not answer the questions by what you think or have always believed. The questions are designed to find out if you understand the material given in the course.

After you have completed each chapter, review the related exam and see how well you know the answers. If you find that you are having difficulty answering the questions, review the material until you think you can answer the questions. It is important that you read the Bible passages referenced as some questions may be based on the Bible text.

How Your Exams Are Graded

Your instructor will mark any incorrectly answered questions. You will be referred back to the place in the course where the correct answer is to be found. After finishing this course with a passing average, you will be awarded a certificate.

If you enrolled in a class, submit your exam papers to the leader or secretary of the class who will send them for the entire group to the Correspondence School.

See the back of the exam booklet for more information on returning the exams for grading.

Why Personal Evangelism?

One of the greatest privileges of the Christian believer is to be associated with God in the important work of winning souls to the Lord Jesus Christ. Few things that we can do are as far-reaching in their consequences. Truly, "the personal worker" affects eternity and will receive eternal rewards (Dan. 12:3).

So closely does God identify Himself with soul winners that He even permits them to speak as if they themselves were able to save souls. For instance, in Romans 11:14, when Paul speaks of saving some of his own people, the Jews, he writes, "If by any means I may . . . save some of them." Again, in 1 Corinthians 9:22, he says, "I have become all things to all men, that I might by all means save some." We all know that Paul himself could not save anyone. Yet God graciously allows him to use this language because of the close way in which He links Himself with the human instruments by whom He furthers His work.

> **Personal evangelism is not only a great privilege; it is also a solemn duty.**

But personal evangelism is not only a great privilege; it is also a solemn duty. The following are but three of many New Testament passages which emphasize the responsibility of each Christian in this matter and the divine plan of worldwide evangelization through the witness of individuals.

The first is the Great Commission, Matthew 28:19-20. Here the Lord commands His disciples to:

- ➤ Go and make disciples of all nations.
- ➤ Baptize them in the name of the Father, the Son, and the Holy Spirit.

observe all that He had commanded.

argue that this command was only intended for a
eople or for a certain period of time. It is the ongoing
ord to everyone whom He has purchased with His

ssage, Ephesians 4:11-12, also teaches the important truth of every-member evangelism. Follow this train of thought: According to verse 11, the ascended Christ gave "gifts" to men. What were these gifts? They were men with divine qualifications for propagating the Christian faith. Some of these men were apostles, some were prophets, some evangelists, some pastors and teachers. Verse 12 tells us why the Lord gave these gifted men—so that, through them, all the saints might be equipped to carry on the work of the ministry, so that in turn the body of Christ might be edified (built up). This is a very important point. The gifts (we emphasize that these are *people*-gifts, not the variety of gifts given to every believer as detailed in Romans 12 and 1 Corinthians 12) were not given so that the saints might sit back, enjoy their ministry, and be perpetually dependent on them. Rather, these men were provided/given for the purpose of training the saints to do the work of ministering. (This, of course does not mean that all believers are expected to be platform preachers, but it does mean that God's purpose for every saint is to be engaged in making Christ known.)

The final passage is found in 2 Timothy 2:2. The apostle Paul, addressing Timothy, writes: "And the things that you have heard from me among many witnesses, commit these to faithful men who will be able to teach others also." The immediate focus of the verse concerns passing biblical truth to others in the church, but it also provides a

> **The Bible uses the process of sowing seed to illustrate the work of evangelism**

principle that we should follow in personal evangelism. Each of us should commit the truth to others, instructing those others to do the same, so that the knowledge of Christ will flow out in ever widening circles, just like the ripples of a pond. Someone has pointed out that there are four generations of Christians in this one verse. How quickly the family can grow! Beginning with one man, if the number of Christians could be doubled each year, there would be 2,147,483,648 believers at the end of 31 years. We see this law of reproduction in nature all around us. In five years, one grain of wheat or rice will multiply to produce thousands of bushels. It is not surprising, therefore, that the Bible very often uses the process of sowing seed to illustrate the work of evangelism (Ps. 126:6; Eccl. 11:6; Matt. 13:1-23).

To summarize, then, we have learned that personal work is:

> A tremendous privilege, affecting eternity.

> A solemn responsibility, involving every Christian.

> The divine method for reaching the greatest number of people in the shortest period of time.

The question each of us must now face is this: *What am I going to do about it?* To anyone who hesitates in responding, we would simply commend the reading of the following paragraph written by an *atheist:*

> *The question each of us must now face is this: What am I going to do about it?*

"Did I firmly believe, as millions say they do, that the knowledge and practice of religion in this life influences destiny in another, religion would mean everything to me. I would cast away earthly enjoyment as dross, earthly cares as follies, and earthly thoughts and feelings as vanity. Religion would be my first waking thought, and my last image before sleep sank me into unconsciousness. I should labor in its cause alone. I would esteem one soul gained for heaven worth a life of suffering. Earthly consequences should never stay my hand, nor seal my lips. Earth, its joys and its griefs, would occupy no moment of my thoughts. I would strive to look upon Eternity alone, and on the immortal souls around me, soon to be everlastingly happy or everlastingly miserable. I would go forth to the world and preach to it in season and out of season, and my text would be—'What shall it profit a man if he gain the whole world and lose his own soul?'"

To conclude this introduction, hear the words of Charles M. Alexander:

"The last thing the devil wants you to do is to win a soul definitely to Christ. If you don't believe, try it. The devil will let you go to prayer meetings, he will let you talk on religious subjects, and do many mighty deeds, if only you will stop short of persuading men to accept Christ as Lord, and openly confess Him before men."

*"May God forbid
That I should meet one soul today
Who through ages of time could say,
I did not point him to the Way."*

Chapter 2

Personal Preparation for Soul Winning

The golden rule for the personal worker may well be found in the words of the Savior, "Follow Me, and I will make you fishers of men" (Matt. 4:19). It is easy to read this verse carelessly and miss its meaning. Notice that it does not say, "Follow a set of rules and you will become a fisher of men." Rather, it instructs us to follow Christ; if we do that, He will "make" us soul winners. In other words, if we are living close to the Lord, if we are walking in fellowship with Him, He will see to it that we will "catch" men. *Our* responsibility is to follow Christ; *His* is to make us fishers of men.

> *Our* responsibility is to follow Christ; *His* is to make us fishers of men.

Very much the same thought is expressed in John 15:4, "Abide in Me, and I in you. As the branch cannot bear fruit of itself, unless it abides in the vine, neither can you, unless you abide in Me." The only way in which a branch can ever bear fruit is by staying so closely connected to the vine that it draws all its strength and nourishment from the vine. In the same way, we can only be fruitful for God as we allow the life of the Lord Jesus to flow into our lives, and through us to others.

It is necessary to emphasize this truth because, although it is not the popular way, it is the only scriptural approach. The temptation today is for the would-be personal worker to disregard his own personal life and simply to depend upon a neat formula, a routine set of questions, human eloquence, a winsome personality, or clever arguments. These may be very appealing and may even seem to produce results, but the fact remains that there is no substitute for holiness of life, for true spirituality. We must begin here, for that is where God begins.

Now if the believer is truly following Christ, or abiding in Him, his life will be marked by certain definite characteristics.

1. First of all, he will be *prayerful*. He will learn what it means to, as it is sometimes phrased, "pray souls into the kingdom" (cf. Rom. 10:1). He will begin each day by making himself available to the Lord—spirit, soul, and body. He will make it a daily habit to ask the Lord for opportunities to witness. He will seek guidance as to the very ones to whom he should speak. Two songwriters of yesteryear have put the desire in prayer form for us:

> *"Lead me to some soul today,*
> *O teach me, Lord, just what to say;*
> *Friends of mine are lost in sin*
> *And cannot find the way.*
> *Few there are who seem to care,*
> *And few there are who pray;*
> *Melt my heart and fill my life,*
> *Give me one soul today."*
> —Will H. Houghton

And:

> *"Lord, lay some soul upon my heart*
> *And love that soul through me;*
> *And may I nobly do my part*
> *To win that soul for Thee."*
> —Leon Tucker

2. He will be *humble*. Instead of seeking to be seen or noticed by others, his goal will be that Christ might be seen in him. John the Baptist exemplified this beautifully. When asked who he was, he replied: "I am the voice of one crying in the wilderness" (John 1:23). A voice is not seen, only heard. John did not want to be seen; he only wanted men to "behold the Lamb of God, who takes away the sin of the world!" (John 1:29).

3. He will be *kind* (1 Corinthians 13:4). He will seek opportunities for doing good to others, so that he might be better able to reach

them with the gospel. It is surely a very one-sided testimony to show no interest in our neighbors except when we speak to them about the Lord. Rather we should minister to them in their need, comfort them in their sorrow, share their burdens, and serve them unselfishly. They will then be much more interested to hear about the Savior we represent.

4. He will *live sacrificially for the spread of the gospel.* The apostle Paul spoke of his willingness to spend and be spent (2 Cor. 12:15). We too should be willing to do without present necessities, to say nothing of comforts and luxuries, in order that souls might not perish for want of the knowledge of Christ, and in order that we might look forward to a harvest of souls (Ps. 126:5-6).

5. He will *have unlimited faith in both the ability and the willingness of the Lord to save sinners.* Like Paul, he will know that the gospel is "the power of God to salvation for everyone who believes" (Rom. 1:16). Like Peter, he will know that God is not willing that any should perish (2 Peter 3:9).

6. Finally, he will *strive to show Christ in all his ways and words.* The example of godly lives plus the confession of godly lips are what is needed by the world today. It should be our desire that Christ should be magnified (exalted) through us (Phil. 1:20).

This raises an important question. Suppose that a Christian is out of fellowship with the Lord. He has backslidden and is cold in heart. Should he let the unsaved know that he is a believer, or would it be better to say nothing about it? Is it possible that such a person might do more harm than good to the cause of Christ by seeking to witness? We would suggest that in order to avoid the slightest possibility of thus bringing reproach on the name of Christ (Rom. 2:24), we should be sure that we are living in daily, hourly, moment-by-moment communion with the Savior.

> **No Christian should ever use his low state of spirituality as an excuse for not witnessing.**

Certainly no Christian should ever use his low state of spirituality as an excuse for not witnessing. His inescapable obligation is to confess and forsake his sin, and thus be restored to the Lord and to a life of usefulness for Him.

In closing, we simply repeat that the great secret of winning souls to the Lord Jesus is to be so yielded to Him and to so abide in Him that He can do the work through us. It is one thing to pray, "Lord, let me win souls for You," and quite another to pray, "Lord, live Your life through me, and thus win souls to Yourself."

Chapter 3

The Soul Winner's Weapon

It is hardly possible to over-emphasize the importance of the Bible in the glorious task of soul winning. The Bible is to the personal worker what a sword is to a warrior (Eph. 6:17) and what seed is to a farmer (Luke 8:11). In short, the Bible is the instrument God uses in the conversion of sinners. In James 1:18 we read, "Of His own will He brought us forth by the word of truth," and Peter wrote that we have been "born again, not of corruptible seed but incorruptible, through the word of God which lives and abides forever" (1 Peter 1:23). Read also Ephesians 5:25-26.

> **The Bible is the instrument God uses in the conversion of sinners.**

The Bible is unlike any other book in the world. "For the word of God is living and powerful, and sharper than any two-edged sword, piercing even to the division of soul and spirit, and of joints and marrow, and is a discerner of the thoughts and intents of the heart" (Heb. 4:12). It can do what no human words can ever do.

How then does God use His Word in the salvation of sinners? First of all, the sinner hears the Word preached, or reads it, or comes in contact with it in some other way. The Holy Spirit of God uses the Word to:

- ➢ Convince the unsaved person that it is indeed the inspired, infallible revelation of God.
- ➢ Convict him of the fact that he is a sinner and that he deserves eternal punishment.
- ➢ Show him that Christ is the Savior he needs (expanded in Lesson 7).

> Lead him to confess his sin, renounce all other hope, and trust implicitly in the Lord Jesus. Thus we read in Romans 10:17, "Faith comes by hearing, and hearing by the word of God." Men receive faith as the Holy Spirit makes the Bible real to them.

Needless to say, the Christian worker must have a proper appreciation of the value of God's Word in order to deal intelligently with souls. We suggest the following:

> *The Christian worker must have a proper appreciation of the value of God's Word in order to deal intelligently with souls.*

1. First of all, he must appreciate that it is not only his best but his only weapon. At various times he will be tempted to use philosophy, reason, and logic to combat the objections of the person with whom he is dealing. To do so would be to throw away his sword and expose himself to the thrusts of the enemy. Very often, worldly men are more adept at scientific arguments than the Christian (Luke 16:8). The soul winner must realize that, as someone has said, "a single verse of Scripture is worth more than a thousand arguments."

   In this connection, it is profitable to remember that the people of the Old Testament were forbidden to sow their vineyards with mixed seeds (Deut. 22:9). The lesson for us is that we should use only the pure, unadulterated seed of the Word of God in dealing with the unsaved, and never mix it with the arguments of science and philosophy. It is futile to go beyond the gospel and discuss deep spiritual truths as the unsaved cannot possibly understand them (1 Cor. 2:14). Instead of arguing about such deep truths as Election, the Trinity, and so on, we need to show the sinner his need of salvation. The unsaved are spiritually blind (2 Cor. 4:4) and cannot see the value of the deep things of God. Their first need is spiritual sight which comes when Christ is received by faith.

2. Second, the soul winner should learn to use the Word extensively. Wise King Solomon wrote, "In the morning sow your seed, and in the evening do not withhold your hand; for you do not know which will prosper, either this or that, or whether both alike will be good" (Eccl. 11:6). Read also Isaiah 32:20.

Ecclesiastes 11:4 states, "He who observes the wind will not sow." The application to the soul-winner is that he should not allow adverse conditions to hold him back. Neither should he stop quoting the Word when he is met with the objection, "I don't believe the Bible is the Word of God." What would a soldier do if the enemy said, "I don't believe your sword is real steel"? He would just give him another thrust and prove its reality! Remind the objector that his unbelief does not alter the truth of the Bible. Then continue to apply the Word under the Spirit's guidance.

3. Next, he should learn to use the Word wisely, in dependence on the Holy Spirit. The verse that God uses at one time may be utterly inappropriate at another. The Spirit of God should be able to use us to quote the very portion of the Bible that He might wish to use.

   This forcefully reminds us of the value of Scripture memorization. The Spirit can only "bring to your remembrance" (John 14:26) what you have previously known. How can I expect the Lord to use me if I have not memorized it? On the other hand, how wonderful it is to be able, at the proper time, to recite the very verse which will bring life and peace and lasting joy to some person.

4. Then we must learn to use the Word with utter confidence that God will bless it. This is one of the great encouragements in Christian work, namely, that the Word of God is never ministered in the power of the Holy Spirit without producing results

> **We must learn to use the Word with utter confidence that God will bless it.**

in hearts and lives. God has promised to honor His Word. "For as the rain comes down, and the snow from heaven, and do not return there, but water the earth, and make it bring forth and bud, that it may give seed to the sower and bread to the eater, So shall My word be that goes forth from My mouth; It shall not return to Me void, but it shall accomplish what I please, and it shall prosper in the thing for which I sent it" (Isa. 55:10-11). Since His Word is as irresistible, invincible, and successful as the rain or snow, let us by all means use it confidently, ever remembering that no such success is promised to our own words.

From all of the above, it should be obvious that since the Word is so necessary, we should have it with us all times. The Christian soldier should never be without his sword. A pocket edition of the New Testament takes up little space or weight, yet how important it is to have it available when an opportunity arises.

Finally, a supply of good gospel tracts is indispensable. Oftentimes they can be handed out when conversation is impossible. The role played by tracts in the salvation of Christians living today is incalculable. Let us not lose out on the blessing resulting from this profitable ministry.

CHAPTER 4

THE MINISTRY OF THE HOLY SPIRIT

In order to be able to deal with souls intelligently, we must be aware of the role of the Holy Spirit in salvation. Such an awareness will deliver us from the twin perils of encouraging false professions and of boasting of our results.

Scripture repeatedly teaches that the new birth is a miraculous, supernatural work of God (John 1:13; 1 Cor. 3:6), and that the Holy Spirit is the Person of the Godhead who brings it to pass (John 3:5).

The Spirit of God is sovereign, that is, He does as He pleases, and is not obligated to give an account of any of His actions (Job 33:13). When the Lord Jesus dealt with Nicodemus, He reminded him that "the wind blows where it wishes" (John 3:8), emphasizing the sovereign and unpredictable nature of the Spirit's activities. This is why, from the divine standpoint, we often find one person saved and the rest of his family lost. It explains why a person like Saul of Tarsus is converted when he least expects it (Acts 9:1-31). It explains why a verse of Scripture that might be meaningless to one person might be the very word used in the salvation of another. It explains why a soul winner can never tell in advance which souls will be saved and which will not.

> The sovereignty of the Holy Spirit does not mean that man has no part to play in his conversion.

The sovereignty of the Holy Spirit does not mean that man has no part to play in his conversion. The Bible teaches with equal clarity and emphasis that man's responsibility is to believe on Christ (Acts 16:31). God offers to save *every* person who receives His Son by faith (John 1:12). Even if we cannot reconcile God's sovereignty and man's free will in our own minds, we should hold both doctrines in perfect balance because both are certainly taught in the Bible.

It is impossible to describe exactly how the Holy Spirit produces the new birth. "You hear the sound of it, but cannot tell where it comes from and where it goes. So is everyone who is born of the Spirit" (John 3:8). However, in general, we can say that He first awakens a real sense of need in the life of a person. (Because of the importance of the subject of conviction of sin, and its apparent neglect today, a separate lesson will be devoted to its study.) Next, He brings him to realize the futility of self-effort. Then, finally, He reveals the Lord Jesus Christ as the One who can satisfy his need.

The Christian worker should always remember that the work of the Holy Spirit must not be usurped. The soul winner's part is to sow the seed and to water it by prayer. The Spirit's part is to produce conviction and conversion.

In his zeal to serve the Lord and to help his fellow men, the Christian is often faced with the temptation to extract a confession from his prospect. Such an effort may be illustrated by the following dialogue:

Question: Do you believe that the Bible is the Word of God?

Answer: Yes!

Question: Do you know that you are a sinner?

Answer: Yes, all men are sinners.

Question: Do you believe that Christ died for sinners?

Answer: Yes, I do.

Conclusion: Then you are saved. The Bible says that all who believe this are saved.

But is the person truly saved? Has the Holy Spirit really worked in his life? Or is this merely an intellectual assent to certain facts? Is it only a false profession? There are three serious dangers in a false profession of salvation:

1. The person might complacently think himself saved, while actually he is in danger of eternal punishment.

2. He might take his place in church fellowship and cause needless difficulty to the people of God.

3. His unsaved acquaintances will expect higher standards of him than he has the power to achieve. Much reproach can thus come on Christ's name through the conduct of false professors.

The personal worker should avoid, therefore, putting pressure on a person to make a profession. The great soul winner, D. L. Moody, wrote: "Never tell a man he is converted. Never tell him he is saved. Let the Holy Spirit reveal that to him." This is especially true in dealing with children, whose minds are susceptible to emotional pleas and high-powered invitations. The New Testament offers no example of prolonged efforts to induce a confession from an individual. Rather, the pattern there is for the Christian to present the gospel faithfully and prayerfully, then look to the Spirit to regenerate the soul. Unfortunately, many modern methods of evangelism arise from a passion to be able to count a large number of converts. This is certainly a shabby motive. Let the soul winner always remember the following:

> *The personal worker should avoid putting pressure on a person to make a profession.*

1. It is quite impossible for us to evaluate the results of our ministry. What is the value of claiming dozens of converts if none of them are truly saved? As has been said, "Heaven will be the best and safest place to hear the results of our work."

2. Very few persons are saved solely through one soul winner. More often there are many links in the chain of salvation. One sows and another reaps. We sometimes reap where we bestow no labor (John 4:37-38).

3. Finally, the number of souls saved through us is not the only measure of our faithfulness. "To the one we are the aroma of death leading to death, and to the other the aroma of life leading to life" (2 Cor. 2:16). In other words, some men hear the gospel from our lips and are saved. Others hear the message, reject it, and perish. Undoubtedly the Lord judges our success as much by the latter as by the former (although we would prefer the former).

To summarize, we would say that the soul winner must remember that only God's Holy Spirit can bring about the new birth; that he should not try to usurp His office by pressing for decisions; that he should not boast of his achievements. It should not make us any less zealous when we realize the key role of the Spirit in salvation, but it certainly should make us more anxious to be dependent on Him and subject to His leading.

Chapter 5

Lessons from the Gospels and the Book of Acts

No treatment of personal evangelism would be adequate without observation of the Master Soul Winner at work. By turning to the gospels of Matthew, Mark, Luke, and John we may travel with the Savior on His missions of mercy and learn many precious lessons from Him on how to deal with souls. The book of Acts also yields profitable instructions on winning souls, for there we see the risen Lord working through His apostles by the power of the Holy Spirit. Needless to say, this lesson can only highlight a few of the many points to be noticed. It is hoped that the student's mind will be thus set in motion to discover additional truths for himself.

First of all, then, let us study the message which the Lord Jesus Christ brought to men and women. We suggest the following five points:

1. Christ emphasized the fact of sin (John 4:16-18). He reached the conscience of the woman at Sychar's well with the straightforward statement, "The one whom you now have is not your husband."

2. Christ emphasized the hopeless condition of the sinner in John 3:6: "That which is born of the flesh is flesh." Since "those who are in the flesh cannot please God" (Rom. 8:8), man, unaided, is doomed.

3. Christ emphasized the necessity of the new birth. Twice in John 3, the Savior asserts that the kingdom of God can only be entered by the new birth. As verse 5 has presented a difficulty to many, we will discuss it briefly here. Water in this verse may refer either to the Word of God or the Spirit of God. Either interpretation is

consistent with the rest of Scripture. (1) The new birth is elsewhere linked with the Word in 1 Peter 1:23 and Ephesians 5:25-26. (2) The water elsewhere in John's gospel refers to the Holy Spirit (John 7:38-39). It would be equally correct to read John 3:5, "Unless one is born of water, *even* the Spirit . . ." (emphasis added). This is a true translation of the original language of the New Testament. To be consistent with the rest of the New Testament, water in this passage could *not* refer to literal water.

4. Christ emphasized the insufficiency of human reason (John 3:12). The truths of the gospel can only be received by faith. They are not contrary to human reason; rather, they are far above it.

5. Christ revealed how the new birth is received (John 3:15-16). The Lord Jesus did not explain to Nicodemus the process by which the Spirit produces the new birth, but rather told him how he could have this glorious birth—simply by faith in the Son of God. Christ always presented Himself as the object of the sinner's faith.

> **Christ always presented Himself as the object of the sinner's faith.**

As we study the methods of the Good Shepherd, we will find additional, practical hints for those who would follow Him in quest of lost sheep. The following five examples may be cited:

1. Christ was always courteous and gentlemanly. He did not break a bruised reed (that is, a burdened soul), nor extinguish the smoking flax (a person with a spark of faith); see Matthew 12:20. It is true that He did not cater to idle curiosity, nor always answer the arguments of hypocrites, but He was accessible to every genuine case of need.

2. Christ condescended to men of lower classes and conditions (Rom. 12:16). He did not let national or social barriers keep Him from a needy soul, for the woman of John 4 was both a Samaritan and an outcast. While He ministered to rich as well as poor, we find that the poor had a special place in His affections. The soul winner should think about this fact deeply and always remember that:

- the poor have the gospel preached unto them (Matt. 11:5)
- God has chosen the poor of this world to be rich in faith (James 2:5).
- not many wise, mighty, or noble men are called, but the foolish, the weak, the base, the despised (1 Cor. 1:26-29).

3. Christ never suggested to men that God needs their talents, their personalities, or their possessions. It is very foolish for Christians to seek to win sinners based on what their prestige or power would mean to God or to the church.

4. Christ used simple, everyday objects to illustrate spiritual truths. As one person has poetically put it, "He talked of grass, and wind and rain; of fig trees and fair weather, And made it His delight to bring heaven and earth together." Likewise, we should train ourselves to see pictures of the gospel in the created universe around us and to use these illustrations in explaining it to others.

> **Christ used simple, everyday objects to illustrate spiritual truths.**

5. Christ kept the conversation from drifting. Both Nicodemus and the woman at the well wanted to change the subject, but He brought them right back to the question of their eternal welfare.

The student will doubtless be able to add many other points to this list, and it will be to his profit to do so. The more he studies the blessed Lord Jesus, the more like Him he will become (2 Cor. 3:18).

Now let us turn briefly to the book of Acts and see the apostles witnessing for the Lord Jesus. There, in a hostile atmosphere, they speak with great boldness concerning the Savior. Two things are noticeable concerning their message.

1. The apostles emphasized the resurrection and ascension of the Lord (Acts 2:24, 32; 3:15, 26; 4:10; 5:30-31; 10:40; 13:30, 33-34; 17:31). They realized that there was no salvation in a dead Christ. But they knew He was alive because they had seen Him after His resurrection. We too, know He is alive, both because the Bible says so and because "He lives within our hearts," as the well known hymn goes.

2. The apostles emphasized the lordship of Christ (Acts 2:36; 10:36), calling upon men everywhere to bow to Him as the rightful and supreme Ruler of their lives. (It is significant to notice that Scripture uses the order "Lord and Savior" [2 Peter 1:11; 2:20; 3:2], whereas we generally say, "Savior and Lord.")

> **The apostles emphasized the lordship of Christ.**

We will do well to follow the early apostles in proclaiming that Christ is a living Person, both God and man, in heaven just now, and that everyone must bow the knee to Him as Lord sooner or later.

CHAPTER 6

CONVICTION OF SIN

Before a person can be saved, he must know he is lost. This is one of the elementary principles of the gospel. The Lord Jesus taught it repeatedly: "Those who are well have no need of a physician, but those who are sick. I have not come to call the righteous, but sinners, to repentance" (Luke 5:31-32). "For the Son of Man has come to seek and to save that which was lost" (Luke 19:10). Now the Bible is emphatic that everyone is a sinner, that all are lost, that each one of us is sick (Rom. 3:23). But not everyone realizes his sinful condition or is willing to admit it. In fact, if left to himself, man would never feel his hopeless condition, thoroughly renounce his sin, or humbly confess it. Only the Holy Spirit of God can so trouble a man concerning his spiritual uncleanness that he will flee to the Savior for forgiveness.

> Left to himself, man would never feel his hopeless condition.

There are two senses in which the Holy Spirit convicts people of sin.

1. First of all, His very presence in the world convicts the world of sin (John 16:7-11). Actually the Lord Jesus Himself should be on the earth, ruling as Lord of all. But He was cast out and rejected. In His absence, He sent the Spirit into the world. The fact that the Spirit is here condemns the world of

    ➢ Sin—because they did not believe on the Savior, but cried, "Away with Him."

    ➢ Righteousness—because Christ went back to heaven, proving that He was right and the world was wrong.

> Coming judgment—because Satan, the prince of this world, has already been judged and condemned. If the leader is doomed, so also are his followers.

2. Secondly, the Holy Spirit works in the hearts of individuals, awakening them to the fact of their spiritual poverty and peril. In some cases, this is a very prolonged time of deep soul trouble. In others, it is a shorter experience, and perhaps not so much of a spiritual upheaval. But whatever its depth or extent, there must be the convicting work of God's Holy Spirit before a soul can be truly led to the Savior.

> There must be the convicting work of God's Holy Spirit before a soul can be truly led to the Savior.

The Bible is full of examples of men who were thoroughly convinced of their own utter unworthiness in the sight of a holy God. Let's consider some.

1. David evidenced conviction with the short statement, "I have sinned against the Lord" (2 Sam. 12:13). Read Psalm 32:3-4 to learn of the physical and emotional turmoil that David went through before he finally confessed his sin.

2. After a long time of trial, Job submitted to the Lord as follows: "I have heard of You by the hearing of the ear, but now my eye sees You. Therefore I abhor myself, and repent in dust and ashes" (Job 42:5-6).

3. When Isaiah had a vision of the Lord, he cried, "Woe is me, for I am undone! Because I am a man of unclean lips, and I dwell in the midst of a people of unclean lips; for my eyes have seen the King, the Lord of hosts" (Isa. 6:5).

4. When Simon Peter became aware that Jesus was no ordinary man, he fell on his knees and said: "Depart from me for I am a sinful man, O Lord!" (Luke 5:8).

5. In Luke 15:17-19, the prodigal son shows the result of the Spirit's work in his life with these words: "How many of my father's hired servants have bread enough and to spare, and I perish with hunger! I will arise and go to my father, and will say to him, 'Father, I have sinned against heaven and before you, and I am no longer worthy to be called your son. Make me like one of your hired servants.'"

Winning Souls the Bible Way

Exam Booklet
AK '10 (1 Unit) WSBW

STUDENT NAME (PLEASE PRINT)

ADDRESS

CITY, STATE, ZIP

COURSE GRADE: _____

INSTRUCTOR

LUKE 24:27

Exam developed by Emmaus Correspondence School, founded in 1942.

A NOTE ON THE EXAMS

The exams are designed to check your knowledge of the course material and the Scriptures. After you have studied a chapter, review the exam questions for that lesson. If you have difficulty in answering the questions, re-read the material. If questions contain a Scripture reference, you may use your Bible to help you answer them. If your instructor has provided a single page Answer Sheet, record your answer on that sheet. This exam contains the following types of questions:

MULTIPLE CHOICE

You will be asked to write in the letter of the correct answer at the space on the right. Here is an example:

The color of grass is

   A. blue   C. yellow

   B. green   D. orange   **B**

TRUE / FALSE

For these questions, circle the correct answer.   (T) F

WHAT DO YOU SAY?

Questions headed this way are designed to help you express your ideas and feelings. You may freely state your own opinions in answer to such questions.

RETURNING THE EXAM

See the back of this exam booklet for instructions on returning your exam for grading.

DO NOT PHOTOCOPY THESE EXAM PAGES

First Printed 2010 (AK '10), 1 UNIT
Reprinted 2014 (AK '10), 1 UNIT
Reprinted 2017 (AK '10), 1 UNIT

ISBN 978-1-59387-120-8

Code: WSBW

Copyright © 2010 ECS Ministries

All rights reserved. No part of this publication may be reproduced or transmitted in any form or by any means, electronic or mechanical.

Printed in the United States of America

CHAPTER 1 EXAM

Why Personal Evangelism?

EXAM GRADE _____

Before starting this exam, write your name and address on the front of this Exam Booklet.

Directions: Read each question carefully and write the letter of the correct answer in the blank space on the right. Use the separate answer sheet if provided.

1. The fact that God uses human beings to bring others to Christ shows
   A. He can't do it Himself.
   B. He wants us to be involved with Him in the task.
   C. He is completely dependent on people because He is spirit.
   D. He wants man to share His glory. _____

2. According to the author, evangelism is the _____ and _____ of every Christian.
   A. privilege / joy   C. responsibility / gift
   B. privilege / duty   D. fulltime work / burden _____

3. The Great Commission was intended for
   A. only the 12 disciples.
   B. the early days of the church.
   C. just the Jewish people.
   D. Christians of all time. _____

4. Ephesians 4:11-12 teaches that
   A. evangelistic work should be done only by pastors.
   B. only those who are so gifted should evangelize.
   C. God's program is mass evangelism by a few preachers.
   D. the purpose of gifted men is to prepare all believers for ministry. _____

5. The principle described in 2 Timothy 2:2 can be equated to
   A. the law of reproduction in nature.
   B. the organizing of church leadership.
   C. the structure of a revival campaign.
   D. the way God gives spiritual gifts. _____

Circle the letter of the correct answer: T—if true, or F—if false.

6. The soul winner can never tell where his influence stops.   T   F

7. Mass evangelism is the most effective way of spreading the gospel.   T   F

8. Christ has provided the church with gifted men to train the church for ministry.   T   F

9. In Matthew 4:19, the Lord Jesus compared soul winning to sowing seed.   T   F

10. Satan doesn't care if Christians are spreading the gospel.   T   F

WHAT DO YOU SAY?

Share briefly about the person(s) God used to draw you to Jesus Christ.

_____

_____

_____

_____

CHAPTER 2 EXAM

Personal Preparation for Soul Winning

EXAM GRADE

Write the letter of the correct answer in the blank space on the right. Use the separate answer sheet if provided.

1. The foundational requirement for winning souls is
   A. remembering to always use tact.
   B. a close and personal walk with the Lord.
   C. following a set procedure.
   D. maintaining enthusiasm and vision. _____

2. When it comes to bearing fruit in our lives,
   A. we must try as hard as we can.
   B. we should go to Bible college to learn how.
   C. God doesn't expect much fruit from us.
   D. we must allow Christ to live through us. _____

3. John the Baptist spoke of himself as
   A. a prophet.   C. a voice.
   B. an evangelist.   D. a preacher. _____

4. Our neighbors will be more open to hearing the gospel from us if
   A. we offer to pray for them.
   B. they see us going to church every Sunday.
   C. we show a genuine interest in their lives.
   D. we keep ourselves to ourselves most of the time. _____

5. Romans 2:24 teaches that
   A. unholy living brings reproach on Christ's name.
   B. we should pray for lost souls each day.
   C. the unsaved overlook our failures.
   D. even backslidden Christians should witness. _____

Circle the letter of the correct answer: T—if true, or F—if false.

6. It is Christ who makes us "fishers of men."   T   F

7. Praying for opportunities to witness for Christ is not necessary.   T   F

8. The personal worker should be prepared to live sacrificially in hope of an abundant harvest.   T   F

9. We know that God is able to save the worst sinner, but we cannot be sure of His willingness to do so.   T   F

10. Being out of fellowship with the Lord excuses us from witnessing.   T   F

WHAT DO YOU SAY?

Write a short prayer confessing any shortcoming that the Holy Spirit has convicted you of in this lesson.

_____

_____

_____

_____

CHAPTER 3 EXAM

The Soul Winner's Weapon

EXAM GRADE

Write the letter of the correct answer in the blank space on the right. Use the separate answer sheet if provided.

1. James 1:18 reads, "Of His own will He brought us forth by _____."
   A. the glory of the law
   B. the word of truth
   C. the preaching of the apostle Peter
   D. the baptism of the Spirit

2. Relying only on the Bible in soul winning, rather than on the Bible plus science, philosophy, or logic is suggested by
   A. Isaiah 32:20.
   B. Ephesians 5:25-26.
   C. Deuteronomy 22:9.
   D. 1 Peter 1:23.

3. Applying the principle about "observing the wind" in Ecclesiastes 11:4, the soul winner will
   A. not allow difficulties to deter him.
   B. only use the Bible with those who are not hostile to it.
   C. use the same Scriptures in every situation.
   D. use the Word sparingly.

4. Memorizing key Scriptures is, to the prospective soul winner,
   A. easy.   C. preferable.
   B. unnecessary.   D. vital.

5. Isaiah 55:10-11 teaches that God's Word is
   A. effective and powerful.
   B. inspired by the Holy Spirit.
   C. eternally true.
   D. going to accomplish what God intends it to.

Circle the letter of the correct answer: T—if true, or F—if false.

6. The Holy Spirit uses the Word to convict people they are sinners.   T   F

7. According to Romans 10:17, every man is born with faith to believe on Christ.   T   F

8. The soul winner should equip himself with strong arguments against evolution.   T   F

9. Quoting the Bible to a man who does not believe it is pointless.   T   F

10. The personal worker should always carry his Bible with him.   T   F

What Do You Say?

Cite at least four verses or passages you would use when sharing the gospel with someone.

_____

_____

_____

_____

CHAPTER 4 EXAM

The Ministry of the Holy Spirit

EXAM GRADE

Write the letter of the correct answer in the blank space on the right. Use the separate answer sheet if provided.

1. When it comes to saving souls, the Holy Spirit
   A. plays no part at all.
   B. determines who will be saved.
   C. endured the cross alongside Christ.
   D. is the agent of the Godhead who effects salvation.

2. The fact that the Holy Spirit is sovereign means that
   A. man's will is not involved in his salvation.
   B. man is not responsible for his eternal state.
   C. He is all-wise and all-powerful.
   D. He acts according to His own good pleasure.

3. How the Holy Spirit produces spiritual birth is
   A. difficult to describe.
   B. clearly explained in Scripture.
   C. only understood by Bible scholars.
   D. not important.

4. A personal worker shows wisdom if he
   A. refrains from affirming to a new convert that he is saved.
   B. works only with children, as they are the most receptive.
   C. presses every evangelistic contact towards a decision.
   D. spends more time evangelizing than praying.

5. The earnest personal worker should strive to
   A. produce conviction of sin.
   B. obtain assent to the facts of the gospel.
   C. present the gospel faithfully and prayerfully.
   D. obtain a profession from every contact made.

Circle the letter of the correct answer: T—if true, or F—if false.

6. Intellectual assent to the facts of the gospel does not save.   T   F
7. False professions can bring reproach on the name of Christ.   T   F
8. It is the person who "reaps" who gets credit from God for the soul saved.   T   F
9. The divine measure of success is the number of souls saved.   T   F
10. Only the Holy Spirit can effect spiritual birth.   T   F

What Do You Say?

Looking back on your own conversion, describe how the Holy Spirit convicted you of your need of salvation through Christ.

_____
_____
_____

CHAPTER 5 EXAM

Lessons from the Gospel and Acts

EXAM GRADE _____

Write the letter of the correct answer in the blank space on the right. Use the separate answer sheet if provided.

1. In Christ's own personal ministry with lost souls, He emphasized
    A. God's love and forgiveness.
    B. the importance of doing good works.
    C. sin, and man's hopeless condition.
    D. that every person is special.

2. Being born of God by the Holy Spirit
    A. is essential to entrance into God's kingdom.
    B. is one way of being saved.
    C. was a special privilege reserved for Jewish believers.
    D. is a teaching found in Matthew's gospel.

3. Christ taught that the means of receiving eternal salvation is
    A. by taking the sacraments.
    B. by obeying the Mosaic law.
    C. by personal faith in Him (Christ).
    D. by giving all one's worldly goods to the church.

4. It is clear from the gospel narratives that the Lord Jesus treated people with
    A. superiority.   C. friendliness.
    B. sternness.   D. courtesy.

5. In explaining spiritual concepts to people, Jesus
    A. used illustrations from everyday life.
    B. limited His teaching to examples from the Mosaic law.
    C. taught everybody the same topics.
    D. only ever taught by means of parables.

Circle the letter of the correct answer: T—if true, or F—if false.

6. Christ gave straight-forward answers to every question people asked Him.   T   F

7. The Lord Jesus limited His ministry to His own national and social circles.   T   F

8. Christ told people that God needs their talents and influence.   T   F

9. In Acts, the disciples limited their message to Christ's crucifixion.   T   F

10. The scriptural order is to accept Christ as Savior, then later crown Him as Lord.   T   F

What Do You Say?

Which of the points made in this lesson will help you in your own ministry of soul-winning?

_____

_____

_____

_____

CHAPTER 6 EXAM

Conviction of Sin

EXAM GRADE

Write the letter of the correct answer in the blank space on the right. Use the separate answer sheet if provided.

1. In Luke 5:31-32, the Lord Jesus taught that
   A. there are some people who are actually righteous.
   B. some good people confess their need of Him.
   C. only those who realize they are sinners can be saved.
   D. He only came to save the best people.

2. The sin of which the Holy Spirit convicts the world is
   A. failure to believe in Christ.
   B. not showing respect for the Bible.
   C. breaking the Ten Commandments.
   D. failure to keep the Golden Rule.

3. Conviction of sin
   A. has to be self-motivated to be genuine.
   B. takes the same form for everyone.
   C. is a work of God the Father.
   D. takes varying forms and length of time.

4. A person has not been completely convicted of sin if he
   A. thoroughly renounces his sin.
   B. acknowledges his own ignorance.
   C. still gives credence to any ritual in achieving salvation.
   D. has an intense longing for salvation.

5. The main lesson for the soul winner in this lesson is
   A. to patiently wait for the Holy Spirit to convict people of their sin.
   B. to begin all evangelistic efforts with presenting Christ as Savior.
   C. to use the same method in every contact he makes.
   D. to urge immediate decisions each time.

Circle the letter of the correct answer: T—if true, or F—if false.

6. The Holy Spirit wants sinners to reform.   T   F

7. David confessed his sin of adultery immediately after committing it.   T   F

8. At Pentecost, Peter pressured the Jews to confess to killing the Messiah that God had promised to send them.   T   F

9. A person who openly opposes the gospel may actually be undergoing conviction of sin.   T   F

10. Conviction of sin will include recognizing no personal merit of salvation.   T   F

What Do You Say?

What steps can you take to ensure that you do not "get ahead" of the Spirit's ministry of convicting individuals?

_____
_____
_____
_____

CHAPTER 7 EXAM

The True Gospel

EXAM GRADE

Write the letter of the correct answer in the blank space on the right.
Use the separate answer sheet if provided.

1. The true gospel includes the teaching that human beings
   A. are saved by leading good lives.
   B. are saved by faith and by doing good.
   C. are saved by faith and kept by works.
   D. are saved by faith alone.

2. To believe that we can save ourselves from sin's penalty
   A. reveals how noble man's heart is.
   B. rob's Christ of the glory He is due for His work.
   C. is taught in Scripture.
   D. was an Old Testament teaching.

3. Sins committed after conversion
   A. disrupt our fellowship with God.
   B. result in our losing our salvation.
   C. need not be confessed to God.
   D. reduce our reward in heaven.

4. According to 2 Corinthians 5:14, the Christian motive for holy living is
   A. fear of the Lord.
   B. a desire to please the Lord.
   C. loving gratitude to the Lord.
   D. hope of reward from the Lord.

5. The believer receives power to live a godly life from
   A. the indwelling Holy Spirit.
   B. a thorough understanding of the Ten Commandments.
   C. the church.
   D. his personal will power.

Circle the letter of the correct answer: T—if true, or F—if false.

6. God deals with us in grace, that is, with kindness we don't deserve. T F

7. The sinner's obligation is to clean up his life before coming to Christ. T F

8. Faith means to take God at His word. T F

9. Christ only died for the sins we committed before we were saved. T F

10. The gospel disregards the standards of the Ten Commandments. T F

What Do You Say?

Explain the gospel in 75 words or less (draft on a separate sheet first).

_____
_____
_____
_____
_____
_____

CHAPTER 8 EXAM

BELIEF AND CONFESSION

EXAM GRADE

Write the letter of the correct answer in the blank space on the right. Use the separate answer sheet if provided.

1. In John 1:12, believing is equivalent to
   A. receiving Christ.
   B. eating bread.
   C. drinking water.
   D. looking.

2. Conversion may be likened to saying "I do" in a marriage ceremony, as in the biblical case of
   A. Esther.   C. Naomi.
   B. Ruth.   D. Sarah.

3. We observe from the healing of Naaman that
   A. faith is linked with obedience.
   B. faith is linked with grace.
   C. faith is linked with works.
   D. faith is linked with baptism.

4. Believing on Christ is
   A. a prolonged and intricate process.
   B. what good people have done from their birth.
   C. not necessary for children of Christians.
   D. an act resulting in the entrance of the Holy Spirit into one's life.

5. Romans 10:10 teaches that
   A. oral confession is necessary for salvation.
   B. a person must know the date of his conversion.
   C. Christ will confess us in heaven.
   D. confession is made of salvation already received.

Circle the letter of the correct answer: T—if true, or F—if false.

6. Placing one's faith in Christ is a deliberate, one-time decision. T F

7. When Christ said He was the Door, He meant we must open our lives to Him. T F

8. Belief in Christ is sometimes similar to unconditional surrender. T F

9. Every genuine salvation can be traced back to a specific date. T F

10. Being baptized is necessary for salvation. T F

WHAT DO YOU SAY?

What is another biblical incident or passage that *illustrates* what it means to believe in Christ?

___
___
___
___

CHAPTER 9 EXAM

The Assurance of Salvation

EXAM GRADE

Write the letter of the correct answer in the blank space on the right. Use the separate answer sheet if provided.

1. For a believer to doubt his salvation at times is
   A. calling God a liar.
   B. a mark of his genuine humility.
   C. a warning to him that he is not truly saved.
   D. understandable.

2. It is accurate to say that
   A. happy feelings are always a proof of genuine salvation.
   B. happy feelings follow assurance of genuine salvation.
   C. the act of trusting in Christ does not affect the emotions.
   D. the act of trusting in Christ prompts some doubts and fears.

3. The Holy Spirit witnesses to believers through
   A. visions.
   B. the convincing words of preachers.
   C. the Bible.
   D. miracles.

4. 1 John 3:14 teaches that
   A. the believer's attitude toward sin changes.
   B. love of other believers is a sign of conversion.
   C. it is presumptuous to say that any one is truly saved.
   D. assurance comes through the Word.

5. When Satan tempts the believer to doubt his salvation, the believer should
   A. ignore him.
   B. think about something else.
   C. quote a gospel promise from the Bible.
   D. rebuke him.

Circle the letter of the correct answer: T—if true, or F—if false.

6. The true salvation experience is always a quiet, inner one. T F

7. The assurance of a godly preacher is as good as the assurance the Bible gives. T F

8. The Christian does not know he is saved because he feels happy, but he feels happy because he knows that he is saved. T F

9. God promises in 1 John 5:13 that whoever has the Son has eternal life. T F

10. A new convert will instantly demonstrate a hatred of sin and desire to please God. T F

What Do You Say?

How do *you* know you are saved?

_____
_____
_____
_____

CHAPTER 10 EXAM

OTHER PERPLEXING PROBLEMS

EXAM GRADE

Write the letter of the correct answer in the blank space on the right. Use the separate answer sheet if provided.

1. In terms of eternity, what matters most is
   A. our family's approval.
   B. our friends' approval.
   C. state approval.
   D. God's approval.

2. A man's faith is only of value if
   A. he places it in a worthy object or person.
   B. he has enough of it.
   C. he has the right kind of faith.
   D. he is sincere.

3. When a convert is troubled by a constant struggle within, he should be taught the biblical teaching of
   A. eternal security.
   B. the unforgivable sin.
   C. baptism.
   D. the two natures.

4. Second Corinthians 5:17 teaches that
   A. Christians stop sinning at conversion.
   B. we should work out our own salvation.
   C. the believer's standing, not his state, is what changes at conversion.
   D. the believer's standing is what he is in himself, not what he is in Christ.

5. The believers at Corinth were told to examine themselves
   A. to see if they were really saved.
   B. as proof that Paul was a genuine servant of Christ.
   C. because Paul wanted them to confess their sin.
   D. to improve their relationship with God.

Circle the letter of the correct answer: T—if true, or F—if false.

6. The teachings of the Lord Jesus cannot be obeyed by the Christian in his own strength.   T   F

7. A person should take his family's feelings into account before trusting in Christ.   T   F

8. Romans 7:15-23 teaches that the believer no longer has any struggles with sin.   T   F

9. The unforgivable sin is using the name of Christ as a curse word.   T   F

10. Living productive lives for the Lord is a life-long choice.   T   F

What Do You Say?

What (genuine) hindrances to trusting Christ have you heard, and how do you (or would you) answer them from the Bible?

_____
_____
_____
_____

CHAPTER 11 EXAM

Follow-Up Work

EXAM GRADE

Write the letter of the correct answer in the blank space on the right. Use the separate answer sheet if provided.

1. The greatest joy of the apostle John's life was
   A. preaching the gospel.
   B. winning souls.
   C. knowing that his converts were growing in their faith.
   D. teaching the Word.

2. First John 2:28 teaches that the life of a convert
   A. will affect his personal reward at Christ's judgment seat.
   B. will affect the reward given to the one who led him to Christ.
   C. is the responsibility of the one who led him to Christ.
   D. has no impact on anyone but himself.

3. In John 21, Jesus conveyed the importance of follow-up work with the command to Peter to
   A. "Feed the flock of God."
   B. "Preach the Word."
   C. "Follow Me."
   D. "Feed My sheep."

4. Having a daily quiet time of prayer and Bible reading
   A. will be an easy practice for the new convert to adopt.
   B. should be taught and encouraged by the worker.
   C. is not as important as attending a church.
   D. is a good work that will gain God's approval.

5. New converts should be urged to
   A. attend the church of their choice.
   B. attend the church of the one who led them to Christ.
   C. attend a church where the Bible is the sole authority.
   D. attend a large church.

Circle the letter of the correct answer: T—if true, or F—if false.

6. Young converts are susceptible to the teachings of false cults. T F

7. The doctrine of eternal security provides a strong motive for righteous behavior. T F

8. Public announcement of a conversion is the responsibility of the soul winner. T F

9. The biblical doctrine of "separation" has three aspects. T F

10. Follow-up is the responsibility of the church most local to the new convert's home. T F

What Do You Say?

Describe your own experience of being "followed up" after you trusted Christ. What have you learned from that?

_____
_____
_____
_____

CHAPTER 12 EXAM

DISCIPLESHIP

EXAM GRADE

Write the letter of the correct answer in the blank space on the right. Use the separate answer sheet if provided.

1. One of the things that "denying self" means is to
   A. adopt a harsh lifestyle.
   B. say no to all forms of entertainment.
   C. realize that I no longer have a free will.
   D. submit oneself to Christ's lordship.

2. New converts learn best how to be a follower of Christ by
   A. following the lifestyle of the one who led them to Christ.
   B. studying what the New Testament teaches on the subject.
   C. going to Bible college.
   D. reading biographies of heroes of the faith.

3. Discipleship is a pathway
   A. to which only certain Christians are called.
   B. which Christians must make a personal choice to follow.
   C. which all believers are treading.
   D. only for those who live in times of persecution.

4. Christianity, according to the New Testament, results in
   A. freedom from danger.
   B. material prosperity.
   C. persecution and hatred by the world.
   D. giving first place to one's family.

5. "Let the dead bury their dead" means that disciples
   A. should not take up the trade of embalming.
   B. should not engage in secular occupations of any kind.
   C. should not touch dead bodies.
   D. should not devote their lives to what the unsaved could do just as well.

Winning Souls the Bible Way

AK '10

Circle the letter of the correct answer: T—if true, or F—if false.

6. It is natural that there will be a time gap between a person's conversion and his becoming a disciple. T F

7. Love for other Christians is one aspect of discipleship. T F

8. A true disciple of Christ will grow in Christ-likeness. T F

9. Love of material comforts is one of the hindrances of being a disciple. T F

10. The Christian's first obligation is to be true to his family. T F

What Do You Say?

Name one aspect of discipleship that you are challenged about, and how you will go about facing it.

_____
_____
_____
_____

WINNING SOULS THE BIBLE WAY　　　　　　　　　　　　　　　　　AK '10

NOW I HAVE A QUESTION . . .

As you complete the exams, you may have additional questions about the course material that have not been answered. On the lines below, you may ask any question you have related to the chapters you have studied. Your instructor will respond to your questions as best as he or she can.

_____

_____

_____

_____

_____

_____

_____

_____

(Leave the below area empty so that your instructor can respond to your questions.)

EXAM BOOKLET

RETURNING THE EXAM BOOKLET FOR GRADING

- ✓ After completing the exam, check it carefully.
- ✓ Make sure you have followed the directions.
- ✓ Be sure you have written your correct name and address on all material you will send to the School.
- ✓ Return all the exams at one time instead of separating and mailing each individual exam.
- ✓ Return only this exam booklet, not the course book. If you have used the single page Answer Sheet, return only that sheet.
- ✓ Address the envelope correctly.
- ✓ Put the correct postage on the envelope.
- ✓ If you are studying this course through an Associate Instructor or associated ministry or organization, send the exams to the individual or organization from which you obtained the course. Otherwise, send them to the address below.

Please return to
Emmaus Bible School UK
Carlett Boulevard
Eastham, Wirral
Merseyside. CH62 8BZ
Tel: 0151 378 7289
www.emmausuk.com

ECS MINISTRIES
The Word to the World

6. The publican was made thoroughly aware of his state before God (Luke 18:13). "Standing afar off, would not so much as raise his eyes to heaven, but beat his breast, saying, 'God, be merciful to me a sinner!'"

7. The Holy Spirit was working in the hearts of men on the day of Pentecost. After Peter had preached to them, "they were cut to the heart, and said to Peter and the rest of the apostles, 'Men and brethren, what shall we do?'" (Acts 2:37). There was no pressure from man. The Spirit did the work.

8. We get a clear indication that the apostle Paul had been convicted of his sin prior to his conversion, because the Lord said to him when He appeared to him on the road to Damascus, "It is hard for you to kick against the goads" (Acts 9:5). Goads were sharp-pointed instruments used to make animals move along. Here they refer to the fact that Paul had been troubled about his sins by the Spirit for some time previously.

9. The Philippian jailer is another case in point. "He called for a light, ran in, and fell down trembling before Paul and Silas. And he brought them out and said, 'Sirs, what must I do to be saved?'" (Acts 16:29-30).

Now we repeat that every person must thus be enlightened as to his lost condition before he will ever feel his need of the Savior. The wise soul winner will ever keep this in mind and will watch for evidences of true conviction. We do not infer that the process itself can always be detected. Sometimes it manifests itself as outright opposition to the gospel, sometimes it appears like nervous or physical illness, sometimes it is seen in bitter weeping, and sometimes it is completely concealed. But the Christian worker can tell when a person has been thoroughly convicted by the following sure signs:

> The wise soul winner will watch for evidences of true conviction.

1. He no longer claims any personal goodness or merit.
2. He thoroughly renounces his sin.
3. He sees no hope in ordinances, rituals, organizations, or men.
4. He has an intense longing for God's salvation (Job 23:3).

It is impossible to point a person to the Lord Jesus until he has been brought to this condition by the Spirit of God. To rush ahead of the Spirit of God and persuade the person to agree to a series of doctrinal statements, however true, is not only worthless, but definitely dangerous, and even sinful.

In this important matter, the wise policy for the worker is to "let patience have its perfect work" (James 1:4). For, "Unless the Lord builds the house, they labor in vain who build it; unless the Lord guards the city, the watchman stays awake in vain" (Ps. 127:1). Let the soul winner be sure that the Spirit is convicting of sin. Let him wait until the Spirit's work is thoroughly completed. Isaiah 28:16 indicates that if the personal worker is really trusting God, he will not be in a hurry. Then let him present the Lord Jesus as the very One to meet the troubled soul's deepest need.

CHAPTER 7

THE TRUE GOSPEL

In order to be an effective workman, the soul winner must know the true gospel message, he must be able to detect false variations of it, and he must be able to answer objections to it.

In his letter to the Galatian church, Paul insisted that there is only one true gospel, and that the curse of God rests upon anyone who preaches another (Gal. 1:8-9). The true gospel, of course, is that salvation is by faith in the Lord Jesus Christ alone (John 14:6). All other gospels or religions may be classified under three broad headings:

> **The true gospel is that salvation is by faith in the Lord Jesus Christ alone.**

1. Man is saved by good works, good character, or human merit of some kind. This might include:
   - Religious rites and ceremonies such as baptism, confirmation, communion, penance, prayers, etc.
   - Keeping the Ten Commandments, or some other rule of life.
   - Good works, gifts of charity, doing one's best.
   - Sincerity, honesty, or fine moral character.
2. Man is saved by faith in Christ *plus* the good works listed above.
3. Man is saved by faith in Christ alone, but in order to remain saved, he must keep performing good works.

All these are conclusively shown to be contrary to God's Word in Romans 4:5: "But to him who does not work but believes on Him who justifies the ungodly, his faith is accounted for righteousness." Read also Galatians 3:3 and 11; Ephesians 2:8-9; and Titus 3:5.

The gospel is the good news that Jesus Christ, the Son of God, died to save men from the penalty of eternal damnation because they could not save themselves, that He rose again, went back to heaven, and now gives eternal life to all who receive Him by faith (1 Cor. 15:1-4).

All idea of man having any merit or power to help in the matter of his salvation is excluded (Rom. 3:27). God looks upon man as dead (Eph. 2:1), and therefore powerless (Rom. 5:6). The thought of meriting salvation appeals to man's heart, but it robs Christ of His glory as the only Savior (Isa. 42:8). Now, in presenting the gospel to the unsaved, there are certain points about which the personal worker should be clear:

1. All men are sinners and are therefore lost. If a person argues that he has not committed the vile sins that others have, we can probably agree. Yet two facts remain:

   ➢ He is *capable* of committing all these sins. Thus, what he *is,* is a lot worse than what he *has done.*

   ➢ If he rejects Christ, he will spend eternity with the most wicked sinners.

Thus to argue that one is good in comparison to others is foolish.

2. "Without shedding of blood there is no remission [forgiveness of sins]" (Heb. 9:22). The personal worker will do well, therefore, to emphasize that Christ shed His blood of infinite value so that sins of deepest depths might be forgiven (1 John 1:7). Emphasize the blood (the sacrificial death) of Christ.

> **The gospel does not end with Christ on the cross; He is a living Savior.**

3. The resurrection and glorification of Christ are of tremendous importance. The gospel does not end with Christ on the cross; He is a living Savior, soon to come for His people; and a living Judge, soon to punish those who do not obey the gospel (2 Thess. 1:8).

4. Salvation is given by God on the basis of His grace (Eph. 2:8). This means that man does not deserve it—he has no claim on God and can do nothing to earn salvation. It means that God saves men

without cause, without hope of being rewarded by men, and without price of any kind. The sinner therefore can come to Christ just as he is, in all his sins, and receive pardon and peace. God does not ask him to reform first or to turn over a new leaf.

5. Salvation is received by man on the principle of faith (Rom. 3:28). This means that man takes God at His word; he believes what God says and acts on it. He takes sides with God against himself. He disclaims any power to save himself or to keep himself saved, but instead casts himself on God's mercy. Faith makes God everything and man nothing.

> **Faith is the means by which man accepts salvation as a free gift from God.**

From this it will be seen that faith is not the savior. Only a living Person can save. Faith is the means by which man accepts salvation as a free gift from God. Faith is not a deserving act or a good work. A man is foolish not to believe God—therefore he cannot boast about his faith. It is the only sane, logical, reasonable response he can make to what we read in God's Word.

6. While good works have no part in obtaining our salvation, they play a major part after we are saved (Titus 2:14). We are not saved *by* good works, but we are saved *unto* (for, to do) good works. Compare verses 9 and 10 of Ephesians 2. Only those who are born again can produce good works in God's sight. They do not perform these good works in order to be saved or to remain saved, but because they *are* saved. All good works performed by Christians will receive rewards at the judgment seat of Christ (1 Cor. 3:12-15).

James emphasizes in his letter that faith without works is dead (James 2:17). Here we see that the faith that saves is the faith that works. True faith produces good works. They are the inevitable result of salvation. If a man is truly saved, he will perform good works.

7. When a person is saved, all his sins are forgiven—past, present, and future. Christ died for all our sins. Sins committed after conversion disrupt our happy fellowship with God, but they do not affect our relationship as children of God. They must be confessed and forsaken before fellowship can be restored.

8. The moment a person is converted, he is as fit for heaven as God can make him. His fitness for heaven depends on the value of Christ's precious blood. Nothing can add to the value of that blood.

9. The Christian has a perfect standing before God because God sees him in Christ, His practical, everyday life should measure up to his exalted standing. When we say that a believer is complete, holy and without blame in Christ, we do not mean that God is not aware of sins in his life. Rather, we mean that God will never condemn him for those sins because the Lord Jesus Christ has already paid the penalty for them.

Now there are three great objections to the gospel of God's grace, all of which the soul winner should know how to answer. The first is this:

1. *"If all you had to do to be saved was believe on Christ, then you could go out and live any way you liked."*

    The answer to this is that when a person is saved, he wants to live a holy life out of love for the One who died for His sins. Love is the strongest of all motives. People will do out of love what they would never do under law. "The love of Christ compels us" (2 Cor. 5:14).

    > **Christians are called to serve, in loving gratitude, the One who died for them.**

    Many well-meaning preachers have felt it necessary to teach that the continued salvation of believers is conditional on a good life in order to keep them in paths of holiness. However, God knows better than man. He gives salvation as a free and unconditional gift, never to be taken back, then asks them to respond to such love by lives of purity and devotion. Christians are called to serve, in loving gratitude, the One who died for them to secure the blessings for them, and who lives to keep them for the blessing.

Then there is this second objection to the gospel:

2. *"If all you have to do to be saved is believe on Christ, then how can you know you will have the strength or power to live as you should?"*

    Such a question overlooks the fact that when a person is saved, he becomes indwelt by the Holy Spirit of God. The Holy Spirit enables him to obtain deliverance from indwelling sin. The true believer has a hatred of sin that he never had before, and a new love for holiness. In addition, the Lord Jesus is ever active to keep the Christian in fellowship with Himself and in separation from evil.

The third prominent objection is:

3. *"If salvation is by faith, then you are saying in effect that the Ten Commandments, originally given by God, are worthless."*

Not at all! The law promised life for obedience, but death for disobedience. We have all broken the law, therefore, we are all guilty of death. The law's demands must be met. The Lord Jesus went to the cross to pay the penalty of the law that we had broken. When we accept Him by faith, the law can no longer condemn us, because its claims have been paid by our Substitute. Thus, "the gospel does not tell of a God whose love has been expressed in winking at sin, but of a God whose love to the sinner could only he expressed where His holy claims against sin were righteously met, and its penalty exhaustively endured" (George Cutting).

In this present day of confused preaching, it is important that the soul winner thoroughly understand the doctrine of the gospel of grace. Only to the extent that he can explain it clearly will he be able to establish young converts in the faith.

Chapter 8

Belief and Confession

In most cases, when a person has a proper appreciation of his own sinfulness and unworthiness, he is not far from the kingdom. The soul winner's task now is to present the Lord Jesus Christ to him as the one who is able and willing to save him, and as the one in whom he should believe.

What does it mean to believe on Jesus? It means to receive Him as personal Lord and Savior by a clear-cut, decisive act of faith. This act of faith need not be oral or public, but it must be heartfelt and sincere.

> To believe on Jesus means to receive Him as personal Lord and Savior by a decisive act of faith.

The Bible uses many different illustrations and examples of what it means to believe on the Lord:

1. Believing is equated to looking, according to Isaiah 45:22. See also John 3:14.

2. In Luke 8:44, a woman touched the hem of Christ's garment, exhibiting faith in Christ's ability to help her in her need.

3. In John 1:12, it is equivalent to receiving Him, welcoming Him, embracing Him. Salvation is likened to a gift which we receive by faith (Rom. 6:23).

4. John 6:35 similarly speaks of Christ as the Bread of Life, to be eaten by hungry souls.

5. The Lord Jesus speaks of Himself as the Door, in John 10:9, which if entered leads to the soul being eternally safe and provided for.

6. In Matthew 8:5-13, the Lord Jesus commends the Gentile centurion for his faith, which he expressed by believing Jesus could heal his servant just by commanding it. The man put his confidence in Christ's authority and power to "save."

It is profitable for the Christian worker to have these and other similes of believing available for use as the occasion requires.

The Holy Spirit uses different ideas or pictures in different cases to bring a person to Christ. No two testimonials of conversion are exactly alike. If we study the experience of Bible characters, we can see how varied they were. Thus conversion might be described as follows:

1. Jacob—struggling against God until God emerges victor (Gen. 32:24-32). In such cases, believing is the same as unconditional surrender.

2. Ruth—finding satisfaction in a person (Ruth 3). Here belief could be likened to saying "I do" in a marriage ceremony.

3. Naaman—obeying a command that seems pointless (2 Kings 5). True trust in Christ laughs at impossibilities and rests confidently in Him. True faith and obedience are inseparable. See 2 Thessalonians 1:8.

> **True faith and obedience are inseparable.**

4. Lazarus—being raised from the dead (John 11:43). For many, belief is simply obeying the life-giving word of Christ, "Come forth!"

5. The so-called "prodigal son"—going home to your father where you belong (Luke 15:11-24). No doubt this description answers to the experience of many wandering souls who have repented, as well as to backsliders.

6. Saul of Tarsus—being suddenly stopped in his tracks (Acts 9:3-4). Here, God's sovereign dealings with man are emphasized. Saul's belief was manifested by his verbal confession of Jesus as Lord (vv. 5, 6).

Whatever the terms used, or whatever belief might be in various instances, it is safe to say that it involves acknowledgment of one's need, a confession of one's inability to meet that need, and a complete reliance on the Savior to do as He has promised.

In connection with the subject of believing, there are two questions which frequently arise.

1. *"Is faith in Christ a definite act or is it a prolonged process?"*

    The answer is that while the steps leading up to conversion may extend over a long period of time, there must be a time when one makes the great decision. This may be demonstrated from Romans 8:9: "If anyone does not have the Spirit of Christ, he is not His." At any particular moment, a man either has the Holy Spirit or he does not have Him. Now, when we are born into the world, we are not indwelt by the Holy Spirit. He takes up residence in us only when we are saved. Thus there must be a definitive time when this takes place. It is foolish for people to say, "I have always believed on Christ." That is equivalent to saying, "I have always had the Spirit of Christ."

2. *"Must I know the date of my conversion?"*

    The answer to this is "No." Many people go through such a time of spiritual turmoil, doubts, and unrest that they do not remember the exact date on which they first yielded to Christ. Where there has been true faith, God knows the date, and that is what counts. The apostle Paul said, "I know whom [not when!] I have believed" (2 Tim. 1:12). The important thing is to know that you are trusting Christ at this very moment.

> **Where there has been true faith, God knows the date, and that is what counts.**

Closely allied to the subject of believing is that of confession. The New Testament does not teach that confession of Christ is essential for salvation, but it does teach that when a person is saved, he will confess his Lord (that is, openly admit to the fact that Jesus is now his Lord).

> ➢ Romans 10:10, "For with the heart one believes unto righteousness; and with the mouth confession is made unto salvation." This is the divine order. First, man believes and is saved. Then he confesses openly concerning the salvation that he has received.

> ➢ Mark 16:16, "He who believes and is baptized will be saved; but he who does not believe will be condemned." While we realize that there is a great difference of opinion concerning this verse,

we suggest the following interpretation. Baptism is here a symbol of the confession which inevitably follows conversion. Therefore, the two are linked together as being closely related. That baptism is not necessary for salvation is shown by the latter part of the verse, "He who does not believe will be condemned," where baptism is omitted. The deciding factor is faith in Christ.

The Savior repeatedly urged His followers to confess Him before men (Matt. 10:32). In dealing with others, we should likewise impress upon them their responsibility to speak out boldly for the Lord.

Chapter 9

The Assurance of Salvation

One of the most common problems that the soul winner will be called upon to deal with is the difficulty so many people have in connection with assurance of salvation. *"How can I know I am saved?"*

There is a widespread opinion that the new birth is always a spectacular and emotional experience, accompanied by mysterious, inward feelings. Since the human heart is forever seeking for signs and miracles and wonders, it is not surprising that it should do so at the time of conversion. Now it is true that in some cases salvation is indeed a stirring event, bringing with it a great emotional upheaval. Such it was with Saul of Tarsus. However, it is equally true that at other times the new birth takes place quietly and without any sensational manifestations.

The point which should be emphasized is that God nowhere declares that we know we are saved because of inner ecstasy or happy feelings we may experience. So many people who actually do believe on the Lord Jesus Christ are disappointed or disillusioned when they do not receive a supernatural sign, either internally or externally. Their difficulty is that they are looking for something which God has never promised.

> **Assurance of salvation comes, first and foremost, through the Word of God.**

The uniform teaching of the Bible is that knowledge (assurance) of salvation comes, first and foremost, through the Word of God. Let us illustrate it in this way. Here is a person who has been brought to the end of himself, has confessed his utter sinfulness and unworthiness, and has definitely called upon Christ for salvation. Yet his feelings have not particularly changed and he is plagued by doubts and fears.

The question is: *"Has that person been born again?"* The answer is, "Yes." Romans 10:13 says, "Whoever calls upon the name of the Lord shall be saved."

"But how can this poor, fearful man know he is saved?" Simply by believing what God has said. God says all who call on the name of the Lord are saved. This man has done so; therefore, he should accept the promise of God that he is saved.

"Even if his feelings do not bear witness to the fact?" Yes, in spite of the evidence of his feelings, he should believe what God says.

If the anxious soul would just stop to think of it, he would realize that there is no better authority in all the world than the Word of God. "Forever, O Lord, Your word is settled in heaven" (Ps. 119:89). "The entirety of Your word is truth" (Ps. 119:160). "It is impossible for God to lie" (Heb. 6:18). Would he rather have some *man* tell him he is saved? That man might be either ignorant or deceptive. Would he rather have happy feelings tell him he is saved? Those feelings might fluctuate from day to day.

But there stands the changeless, infallible Word of God, offering the strongest possible assurance that all who have believed on Christ are saved for eternity. Nothing could be more conclusive than this. It is said that Martin Luther was once asked, "Do you feel that your sins have been forgiven?" His reply was, "No, but I'm as sure of it as that there is a God in heaven."

> *"For feelings come and feelings go,*
> *And feelings are deceiving.*
> *My warrant is the Word of God,*
> *Naught else is worth believing."*

It is an insult to God for a person who has put his faith and trust in the Lord Jesus to doubt his salvation. God says that those who trust Christ are saved. To disbelieve God is to accuse Him of lying. "He who does not believe God has made Him a liar" (1 John 5:10). "Let God be true but every man a liar" (Rom. 3:4).

We have said previously that we do not know we are saved by happy feelings. However, it should not be inferred from this that salvation has nothing to do with the emotions or that a person who knows he is saved should not feel happy. Such is not the case. All who put their trust in Christ should indeed rejoice (Ps. 5:11). But the great and important point is that a person cannot feel happy about his salvation until he first knows that he is saved, and he will never know he is saved until he believes the testimony of the Word of God.

As a believer reads and accepts the Bible, the Spirit of God witnesses to him that he is now a child of God (Rom. 8:16; 1 John 5:10-13). For instance, as I read John 6:47, the Spirit of God tells me that I have everlasting life. I have believed on Christ, therefore, the rest of the verse must be true—I have eternal life. I am filled with the happiest emotions and the deepest peace because I know I am saved.

> After a person has been saved, he receives other evidences of the new life.

After a person has been saved, he receives other evidences of the new life. He knows he has passed from death to life because he loves his Christian brethren (1 John 3:14). He finds that he has new tastes, new desires, and new ambitions. He has a new horror of sin, and a fear of displeasing his Lord. But these are not always evident at the instant of conversion. The first and immediate means of assurance is the Scriptures.

When the personal worker contacts someone who is troubled with doubts and fears, he should recommend that person read his Bible. When the Lord Jesus was tempted by Satan, He quoted Scripture and Satan fled. So when the enemy casts doubts in the Christian's mind, the Christian should quote a gospel verse promising life to everyone who believes in Christ. He is thus saying in effect, "God says I am saved; and I don't care what you say."

Sometimes the soul winner will meet those who count it a sign of humility or godliness to doubt their own salvation. He should remind them that if they have actually received God's Son, they are dishonoring the majesty of His throne by doubting His promise. Persons in poor health or in advancing years often doubt their salvation, but that is a different matter. The Lord knows all about it, and His promise stands in spite of the sickness of the frail human mind.

For many people, assurance of salvation comes like a second conversion. One of the great rewards of the soul winner is to see the joy and peace that comes to those who rest on God's Word for the knowledge of sins forgiven. It is worth more than the world can offer.

CHAPTER 10

OTHER PERPLEXING PROBLEMS

It is impossible in any study on the topic of personal evangelism to cover all the hindrances that individual souls wrestle with in connection with trusting Christ for salvation. However, the great majority of these difficulties follow a general pattern, and if the soul winner knows how to deal with the major questions, he can usually be of real help to the anxious.

In this lesson, we will discuss some of the more common questions that arise in people's minds. The first is this:

1. *"I would like to be saved, but I feel very sure that I would not be able to live the life!"*

    Usually this is the expression of a very sincere, conscientious type of person who realizes that where there is true faith in Christ, there is also a changed life. What this person doesn't realize is that with the new life comes new power. The Holy Spirit enables the believer to live the Christian life. Actually, no man, saved or unsaved, has the strength to live up to the teachings of the Lord Jesus by himself. They call for supernatural power, and this is just what is put at the believer's disposal the moment he trusts the Savior.

    > No man, saved or unsaved, has the strength to live up to the teachings of the Lord Jesus by himself.

Another common problem is this:

2. *"My difficulty is that I fear what relatives and friends will say if I were to go back and tell them I am saved."*

Too often this issue is not put into actual words by the anxious soul, although it is the very thing that keeps people from Christ. The Christian worker must seek divine help in diagnosing the difficulty and prescribing the remedy. Apparently the Savior knew that many would be ashamed of Him for He said, "Whoever is ashamed of Me and My words, of him the Son of Man will be ashamed when He comes in His own glory, and in His Father's, and of the holy angels" (Luke 9:26).

For any who are troubled with this, the personal worker might suggest the following:

> **The approval of God is more important than the esteem of men.**

- The approval of God is more important than the esteem of men. One hundred years from now your friends' opinions will mean nothing, but God's approval will mean everything.

- It is utterly absurd for puny men to be ashamed of their Creator and Redeemer. He was not ashamed to die for sinners; why should sinners be ashamed to live for Him?

- The best thing to do is to place your trust in Christ, then seek by God's grace to win your mocking relatives and friends to Christ. Often, those whose scorn we fear most are the ones who actually are most respectful of a bold stand for the Lord.

Another concern relates to the matter of believing correctly:

3. *"As far as I know, I have really believed on Christ. But have I believed correctly? Did I have the right kind of faith? Or the right amount?"*

This anxiety arises from thinking too much about one's faith rather than upon the Person on whom that faith is resting. A man might have tremendous faith in an unworthy object, and be thoroughly disappointed. On the other hand, it is impossible for anyone to have faith in the Lord Jesus and ever regret it.

Thus the soul winner can answer this type of difficulty as follows: If your only hope for heaven is in the Lord Jesus Christ, you have believed right. If your trust is in Christ, you can never be wrong.

George Cutting, in his book "Light for Anxious Souls," answered this type of inquirer as follows:

"Do you believe

> that you are totally 'without strength'—perfectly helpless as to meeting the question of your guilt and sin?

> that Christ alone by His sacrificial death can save you?

> that God has righteously given to Him sin's full judgment when in love He gave Himself to be made sin for us?

> that God has declared His satisfaction in that sin-atoning sacrifice by raising Him from the dead and crowning Him with heavenly glory?

> that you called upon Him in the sense that without Him you are forever undone and that He is ready and willing to save you?

Then take the sweet assurance which His own faithful Word affords that salvation is yours. Do not hesitate to confess it, nor longer withhold the praise that is due to Him for it."

The new convert is often troubled by this issue:

4. *"I have trusted Christ, but would I have such a struggle within if I were truly saved?"*

The answer is, "Yes." The struggle within really begins when you are saved, for it is then that you receive a new nature which, from that time on, is always at war with the nature you were born with, your sinful nature. This struggle is described in Romans 7:15-23. God wants the new nature to have the victory, and so gives us His Holy Spirit. As we yield to the Spirit and allow Him to have His way, moment by moment the old nature is kept in the place of death to which God has sentenced it (Rom. 6:6-11).

Then there is this familiar query:

5. ***"I worry that I might have committed the unpardonable sin."***

Answer: If you have committed it, you probably wouldn't be worrying about it or have a troubled conscience about it. The unpardonable sin is saying that the miracles of Jesus were performed by the power of the devil rather than by the power of the Holy Spirit, and is the testimony of the forever-hardened heart. The sin that you should worry about is that of rejecting Christ. Those who die in unbelief are forever lost.

> **Those who die in unbelief are forever lost.**

In addition to the above problems, there are two or three verses of Scripture which, when wrongly applied, have caused distress to persons longing for assurance. The first is 2 Corinthians 5:17:

"Therefore if any man be in Christ, he is a new creature: old things are passed away; behold, all things are become new."

When new converts find that all the old habits, evil thoughts, and wicked desires do not immediately cease at the time of conversion, they begin to fear that they are not new creatures after all.

The confusion arises from the fact that this verse describes our *standing*, not our *state*. The key to the verse is found in the words "in Christ." As God sees us in His Son, old things such as guilt and condemnation have passed away, and our position (standing) in Him is entirely new. God expects old things in us to pass away too, and for our lives to be changed practically, but this does not take place immediately. Our standing is complete at the time of conversion; our state should increasingly measure up to it.

A second verse that sometimes bothers young Christians is 2 Corinthians 13:5:

"Examine yourselves as to whether you are in the faith."

People say, "That's just the trouble. The more I examine myself, the more I fear I am not saved."

This is an example of what happens when a verse is separated from its context. The situation in Corinth was that some of the church there were doubting Paul's authority as an apostle. They were asking for some proof that Christ was speaking through him. So he answers in verses 3 and 5,

"Since you seek proof of Christ speaking in me . . . examine yourselves as to whether you are in the faith." They themselves had been led to Christ by him, and were therefore living proof of His authority and authenticity. Paul did not tell them to look within for proof of their salvation; he would have pointed them to the Scriptures for that. On the other hand, there were (and are) many who are only professing believers in Christ, and these need to be challenged as to the reality of their faith.

One final verse that deserves consideration is Philippians 2:12:

"Work out your own salvation with fear and trembling."

At first sight, this seems to teach that salvation is something we produce ourselves. However, it is not the salvation of the soul that is in view, but rather the salvation of the life career, the life lived on earth. It is possible for a person's soul to be saved, and yet for his life here on earth to be wasted or lost. Paul here exhorts the Philippians to be sure that the remainder of their lives here on earth were lived for the Lord by allowing God to work out His good pleasure in them (v. 13).

> It is possible for a person's soul to be saved, and yet for his life here on earth to be wasted or lost.

As has been said, those are just samples of the difficulties which the personal worker will meet. His best equipment for answering them will be an accurate familiarity with the Bible and a humble dependence upon the Holy Spirit.

CHAPTER 11

FOLLOW-UP WORK

One of the most important phases of the personal evangelist's ministry is what is known as follow-up work; yet, strangely enough, it is one of the most neglected fields today. The tremendous significance of this ministry may be judged from the following:

1. The apostle John, writing by divine inspiration, said that his greatest joy was to hear that his converts were walking in the truth (3 John 4). Even greater than the joy of leading souls to Christ is the subsequent satisfaction of seeing them go on well.

2. There is the strong suggestion in the apostle John's writings that the Christian worker will be ashamed at the judgment seat of Christ if his converts have not advanced in the things of the Lord: "And now, little children, abide in Him; that, when He appears, we [that is, the apostles] may have confidence and not be ashamed before Him at His coming" (1 John 2:28). Read also 2 John 8: "Look to yourselves, that we [the apostles] do not lose not those things we worked for, but that we may receive a full reward."

> Even greater than the joy of leading souls to Christ is the subsequent satisfaction of seeing them go on well.

3. Follow-up is not optional, but is directly commanded in the Scriptures. The directive to elders in 1 Peter 5:2 to "Shepherd the flock of God" implies that the sheep need care and supervision.

4. In John 21:15-17, Jesus asked Peter three times if he loved Him. When Peter answered in the affirmative three times, the Lord commanded him to feed His lambs and sheep. In other words, one

of the greatest ways we can show our love to the Lord Jesus is by caring for His own.

5. Young converts are particularly susceptible to the teachings of false cults, and the earnest personal worker should certainly strive to save them from these damnable heresies (1 John 2:18-27).

6. Finally, we should be vitally interested in saving the young in the faith from going back into the world and from bringing shame on the testimony of the Lord Jesus.

With this in mind, we would suggest the following practical steps to be taken by the soul winner.

1. Whenever possible, get the name and address of those with whom you deal. This will enable you to visit them, or, where this is impossible, to carry on a helpful correspondence.

2. Make sure that every convert has their own copy of the Bible, or at least a New Testament. It is absolutely necessary for growth. (We suggest that you enroll new converts in the ECS courses like *What the Bible Teaches*, *Lessons for Christian Living*, or *The Christian Life*. Also, keep a supply of helpful booklets to give to new converts that they may be established in their faith.)

3. Try to be certain that the young believer is thoroughly grounded as to assurance of salvation. Since this subject has been discussed in detail in Lesson 9, we will not repeat it here. In their early enthusiasm and joy, young Christians are apt to parade their assurance unwisely, giving the impression, unintentionally, that they are superior to others.

4. By all means, teach the young in the faith to obey the Lord in the two ordinances of the church, baptism and the Lord's Supper.

5. Teach the new believer the precious truth that in Christ he is safe evermore, using such passages as John 10:27-29; John 5:24; John 3:36; Romans 8:38-39; and Jude 24. Here again, however, balance is needed. Emphasize that the Christian's security is not license for him to live carelessly, but rather it should provide the strongest motive for godly behavior.

> **The Christian's security is not license for him to live carelessly.**

6. Encourage him to confess the Lord before others (Rom. 10:9). In this connection, it is a wise policy to let the new convert announce his faith in Christ to others rather than have the personal worker do it. After all, there can never be any progress in divine things for those who are unwilling to confess Christ.

7. Show the babe in Christ how to set aside a time each morning for the reading of God's Word, for meditation, and for prayer. This is a tremendously difficult discipline for many people. They are apt to become discouraged by constant failure. Yet the daily quiet time is so important that the personal worker should exert great effort to see that it is observed by his converts.

8. Teach the new believer the importance of church fellowship. Remind him that the church is the means through which God chooses to work in the world today (1 Tim. 3:15). Show him that preaching the gospel was only one of Paul's aims; the other was to ground his converts in the truth of the church (Eph. 3:8-9).

The practice of encouraging new believers to join the church of their choice is absurd. Their choice might be directly contrary to the Bible. They should rather be guided to a fellowship where Christ is the acknowledged Head, where the Word of God is recognized as the only authority, and where the Holy Spirit is allowed to lead the worship and service of God's people.

9. Emphasize the two sides of the truth of separation: separation *to* God, living purposefully for His glory, and separation *from* worldliness, from ungodly associations.

10. Show the importance of good works in the Christian's life. The testimony of a person who obviously lives for others is a powerful argument to the unsaved.

11. Impress upon each believer his responsibility to win others for Christ. Help him to understand that God wants the combined witness of a godly life and consecrated lips.

Obviously there are many more matters with which the young Christian should be acquainted. The entire teaching of the Bible is the subject of follow-up work. However, the above points are listed in an effort to show the soul winner the general type of information which should be covered at the earliest possible time.

Chapter 12

Discipleship

In winning souls to Christ, one of the great perils is that the converts might stop short of full discipleship. Too many are content to accept Christ as Savior and then be quite unwilling to follow Him passionately and devotedly, whatever the cost may be. Even a casual reading of the Gospels shows that Christ does not call men to lives of comfort, prosperity and popularity. Rather, He sets forth the sternest demands on those who would be His disciples. The Christian worker should, therefore, earnestly seek to instill a mindset of following Christ fully. At the very least he should try to eliminate what has become a customary "gap" between conversion and consecration. The following are the marks of Christian discipleship:

> *The Christian worker should earnestly seek to instill a mindset of following Christ fully.*

1. A willingness to deny one's self, to take up one's cross, and follow Him (Matt. 16:24).

    - To deny self means to deny that self has any rights, to submit self wholly to the will of Christ.

    - To take up one's cross means to die to sin's appeal, to self's claims, and to the world's applause. The cross meant shame, suffering, and death for the Lord. It was the place where God condemned and punished sin, so we should adopt the same attitude to it.

    - To follow Christ means to go where He wants us to go, wherever it may be, and whatever the cost.

2. A steadfast abiding in the teachings of Christ (John 8:31). This means a profound submission to the will of our Lord at all times (1 John 3:24).
3. A love for Christ that makes all other love seem like hatred in comparison (Luke 14:26).
4. A love for other Christians (John 13:35). It is useless to talk about loving God if we do not love His people (1 John 4:20).
5. A life of fruitfulness to God (John 15:8). This means not only zeal in service, but more particularly, growth in likeness to Christ and in dependence on the Holy Spirit to live for Him.

> Discipleship is a pathway which the Christian can choose or refuse.

Now, it is possible to be a believer in the Lord Jesus and yet not be a disciple. Discipleship is a pathway which the Christian can choose or refuse. It begins with a definite act of committing oneself to Christ, then continues in a daily experience of yielding to Him (Rom. 12:1-2).

Discipleship means *the hatred of the world* (Luke 6:22; John 15:18-21; 17:14). It means *persecution* (Luke 10:3; John 16:1-3; 2 Tim. 3:12). It means *ridicule* (1 Peter 4:4). It means *loneliness,* walking through the world as pilgrims and strangers (John 17:16; 1 Peter 2:11). It means *living sacrificially for the spread of the gospel* (Acts 20:24; Phil. 3:8). It may mean *poverty* (2 Cor. 11:27). It means, in short, living for the Lord Jesus Christ alone (Matt. 6:24).

There are three great hindrances to true discipleship, which are graphically pictured for us in Luke 9:57-62.

1. The first is *material comforts.* "Now it happened as they journeyed on the road, that someone said to Him, 'Lord, I will follow You wherever You go.' And Jesus said to him, 'Foxes have holes and birds of the air have nests, but the Son of Man has nowhere to lay His head'" (vv. 57-58).

    This man expressed willingness to follow the Lord anywhere. In reply, the Lord reminded him that it might involve being poorer than the foxes or the birds. This is the last we ever hear of the man. He did not think the cost of following Christ was worth it. Converts should be taught that discipleship must mean willingness to give up modern appliances, comfortable furniture, and well-equipped homes. They might have to look on and see young Christian friends prospering materially while they deliberately sacrifice to send money to missionaries or to go themselves with the gospel.

2. The second great hindrance is a *job* or *occupation*. "Then He said to another, 'Follow Me.' But he said, "Lord, let me first go and bury my father.' Jesus said to him, 'Let the dead bury their own dead, but you go and preach the kingdom of God'" (vv. 59-60). This man had a job to do. He wanted to bury his father. This was a perfectly respectable thing to do, but it should not have hindered his discipleship. The man said in effect, "Lord . . . me first," and thereby showed that he was not qualified to follow the Lord.

The Lord's answer is most revealing. "Let the dead bury their own dead, but you go and preach the kingdom of God." In other words, there are certain jobs which even the spiritually dead can do, such as burying the dead, but there are other jobs which only a Christian can do, such as preaching the kingdom of God. We should not spend our lives doing what the unsaved can do.

> **We should not spend our lives doing what the unsaved can do.**

The passage does not mean that Christians should not have secular occupations. However, our job should not be the great aim of our existence. We should not live simply to purchase food and clothing. Rather, our main aim should be to make Christ known, and our job should be secondary. God has already promised to provide food and clothing for those who put His cause first (Matt. 6:33). Missionary to India William Carey said his business was to preach the gospel, and he repaired shoes to pay expenses.

3. The third hindrance is *family* or *social ties*. "And another also said, 'Lord, I will follow You, but let me first go and bid them farewell who are at my house.' But Jesus said to him, 'No one, having put his hand to the plow, and looking back, is fit for the kingdom of God'" (vv. 61-62). This man started out to plough, but then remembered his friends and turned back. The Lord said in effect, "My disciples are made of sterner stuff than that."

Thus discipleship involves steadfastness and stability. Weeping mothers and fathers and socially ambitious relatives have deflected many young converts from following Christ. The unwise advice of friends, "You have your future to think of," has turned others aside.

Young believers must be taught that the claims of Christ come first. They must be cautioned not to judge true Christianity by what they see around them, but rather to go back to the New Testament to learn what it really means to be a follower of the Lord Jesus. They must be shown that only as they are willing to spend their lives in service for Christ will they bring life to others and find eternal gain for themselves (John 12:24).

> **Believers must be taught that the claims of Christ come first.**